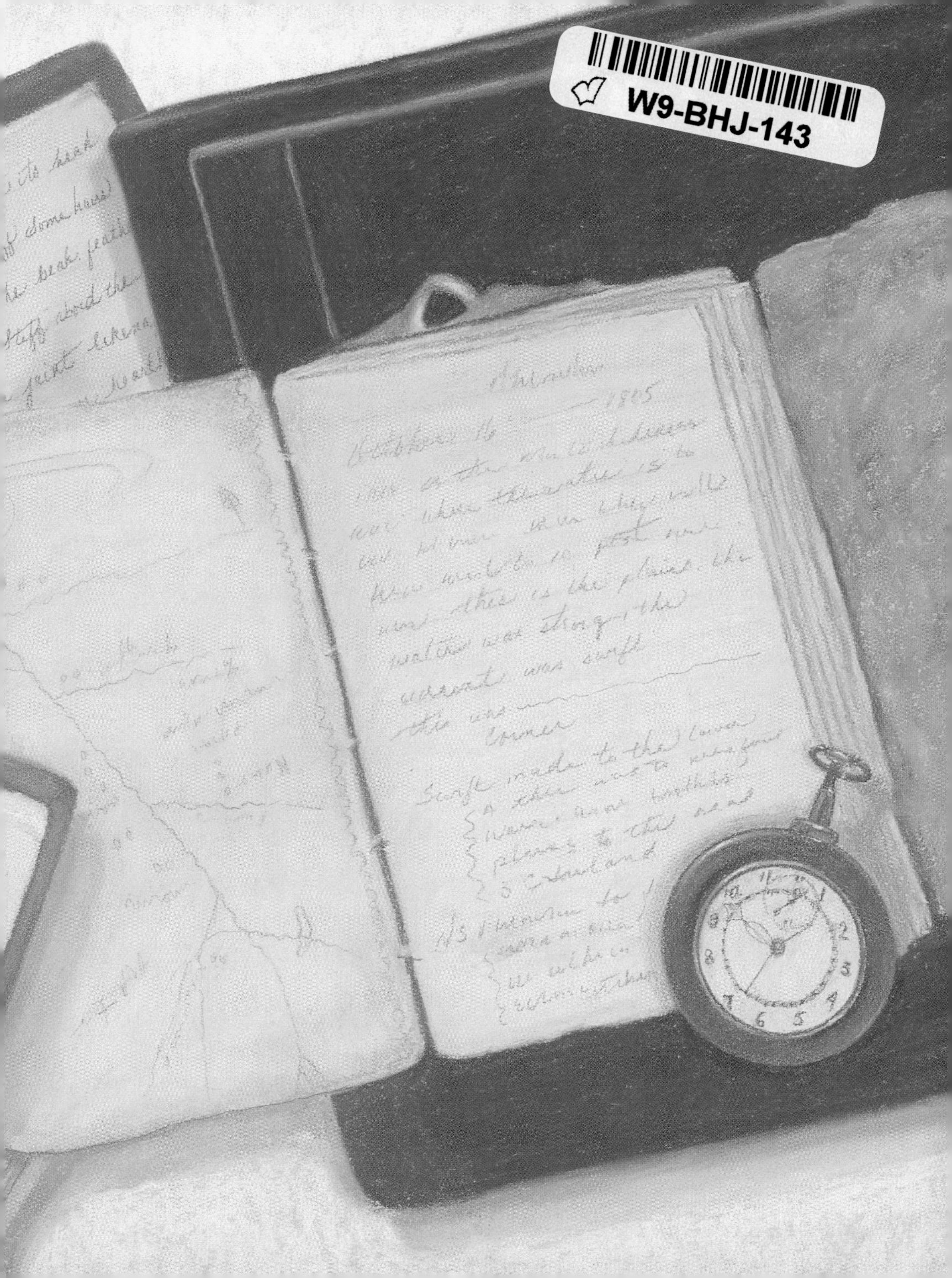
1805

Creative Director: Susie Garland
Art Director: Pat Thompson
All art and editorial material is owned by Dalmatian Press.
ISBN: 1-57759-384-7

The DALMATIAN PRESS name, logo and spotted design are
trademarks of Dalmatian Press, Franklin, Tennessee 37067.

11038a/Sacagawea's Story

00 01 02 03 LBM 10 9 8 7 6 5 4 3 2 1

SACAGAWEA
Lewis and Clark's Shoshone Guide

Written by Cindy Robertson
Illustrated by Pat Thompson

In the early 1800s, the states west of the Mississippi River were uncharted lands owned by France and Spain. Many Native tribes inhabited these lands. The only white men the Native Americans had contact with were fur trappers and missionaries. The tribes traded fur pelts for guns and other supplies.

The United States purchased from France in 1803 a large expanse of land stretching from the current state of Louisiana

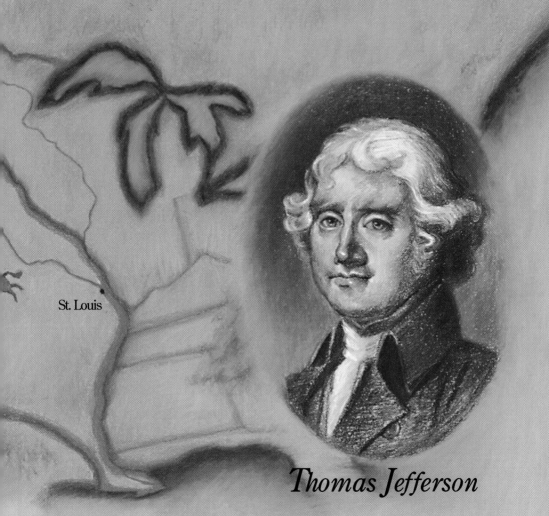

St. Louis

Thomas Jefferson

to the Montana/Idaho border with Canada. The government paid $15 million for 524,800,000 acres of land - that is about 3 cents per acre. President Thomas Jefferson wanted to know about the Native tribes, rivers, plants and animals that were found in this new frontier land. Jefferson asked his friends, Meriwether Lewis and William Clark, who had served together in the Army, to put together an expedition of volunteers to explore the Louisiana Purchase.

On May 14, 1804, the group of 45 men left the settlement of St. Charles on the Missouri River in keelboats and headed into the unknown land of the Native tribes and the buffalo. Captain Lewis took his large black Newfoundland dog, Scannon along on the trip. Scannon was a great watchdog, hunter and companion. Each night the expedition would make camp. Around the campfire, they would enjoy their dinner and talk about what adventures they would have as they traveled to the Pacific Ocean.

In November the explorers reached the village of a native tribe called the "Mandans" in what is now the state of North Dakota. The Mandans lived in earthen lodges. The men were great hunters and the women were skilled farmers. Lewis and Clark decided to spend the winter with this tribe.

To travel across the Rocky Mountains and reach the Pacific Ocean, the group would need horses and guides. The Mandans told Lewis and Clark that the Shoshone tribe who lived near the Rocky Mountains (in the current state of Idaho) had horses. The Mandan said the Shoshone could also provide guides through the mountains.

During their winter in North Dakota, Lewis and Clark
met a French fur trapper Toussaint Charbonneau, who was
married to a young Shoshone girl named Sacagawea. In the
Shoshone language her name meant "Bird Woman."

When the expedition set out for the Rocky Mountains in the spring, Charbonneau, Sacagawea, and their baby boy, Jean Baptiste, went with Lewis and Clark. Sacagawea was happy to be returning to the land of the Shoshone. At the age of eleven, a raiding party of the Hidatsu tribe had kidnapped her from her village. After living with the Hidatsu for about four years, the Hidatsu chief sold Sacagawea to Charbonneau. Sacagawea then became Charbonneau's wife.

Lewis and Clark kept journals during the expedition. They wrote about the trip and made drawings of plants and animals they saw along the way. During their trip, 122 species of animals and 178 species of plants were documented and recorded in the journals. They gave Sacagawea and her baby nicknames because their real names were hard for Lewis and Clark to pronounce and write down. Sacagawea was called "Janey" and Jean Baptiste was known as "Pompey." Sacagawea once saved the journals when the canoe she was riding in tipped over and the journals fell into a rain-swollen river.

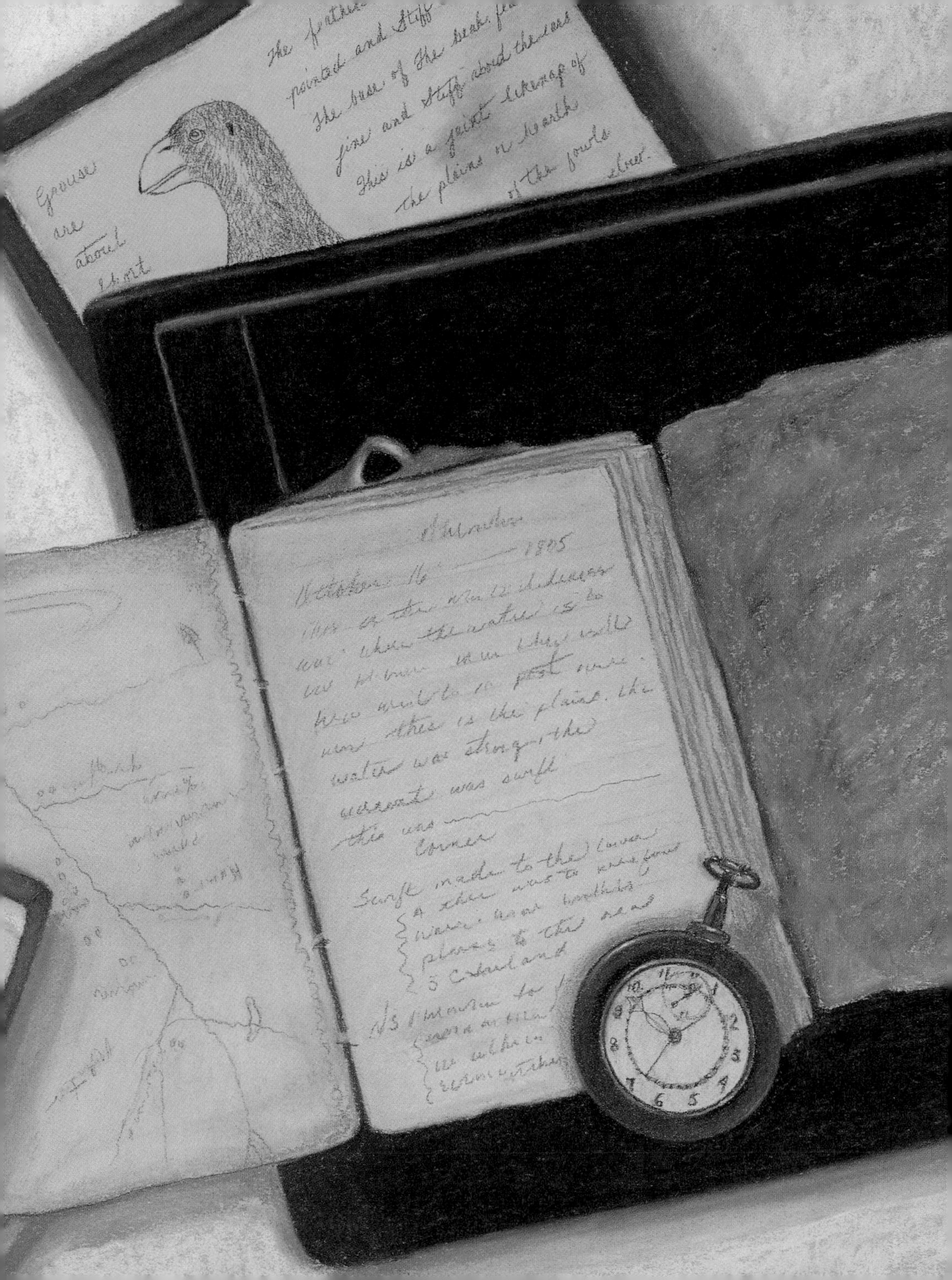

Late in July Sacagawea's cry of joy announced the group's arrival at the Shoshone village. Sacagawea was so happy to see her family and friends again. When she was invited to join the meeting with the leaders of the tribe, Sacagawea let out another cry of happiness. The Shoshone chief was her brother, Cameahwait. She explained to her brother that the group would need horses and a guide through the mountains. The Shoshone sold horses to the expedition and sent an old man whom Lewis and Clark called "Toby" to guide them through the rugged mountain passes of the Rockies.

The mountain passes were the roughest part of the trip. Wet, slushy snow fell making it hard for the people and horses to walk along the narrow ridges. Food supplies ran very low on this part of the trip. Sacagawea showed the men berries and roots that were safe to eat.

As the group traveled through various Native American villages (who had little contact with white men), they were

greeted as a peaceful expedition because war parties did not travel with a women and a baby. Even though Sacagawea did not translate or speak all the languages of the tribes the group encountered, she could communicate with them using Native American sign language.

The expedition reached the Pacific Ocean in November of 1805. Everyone was fascinated by the beach and the animals and sea creatures that lived there. Think of what Sacagawea felt as she saw the "Big Water" for the first time! She tasted the saltiness of the water as it sprayed on her face and marveled at the vastness of the ocean. She loved the feel of the sand under her feet and the way it sifted through her fingers as she scooped up seashells. She brought her young son, "Pompey" to the beach to see the "Big Water."

The group built a fort out of logs on the Oregon coast and spent the winter there. In March of 1806, they began the long trip back to St. Charles. Sacagawea and her husband left the expedition when they returned to the Mandan village. Clark promised Sacagawea that he would provide young Pompey with a good education if Sacagawea would let him come live with Clark. When Pompey was older, he moved East to live with Clark, who cared for him just as he had promised. Pompey returned to the West as a grown man and became a famous guide.

There are different stories about what happened to Sacagawea. One story says she died of a fever at the age of

25 leaving an infant daughter and her son, Pompey. Another more pleasant story says Sacagawea returned to the Shoshone, where she was a well-respected member of her tribe and lived to be almost 100 years old.

Sacagawea was only 15 years old when she joined the Lewis and Clark expedition. She made the long, difficult trip with her infant son to care for. Her bravery, maturity and intelligence helped guide the Lewis and Clark group safely and successfully. The Lewis and Clark expedition began America's growth as a nation by opening the Western states for settlement.

SACAGAWEA DOLLAR

Beginning in the year 2000, the Sacagawea Dollar will be minted in Philadelphia and Denver to replace the Susan B. Anthony Dollar which has been in circulation since 1979. The Sacagawea Dollar features a unique gold color. The coin has a pure copper core with outer layers composed of 77% copper, 12% zinc, 7% manganese and 4% nickel. The coin is 26.5 mm in diameter with a weight of 5.670 grams and a thickness of 1.75 mm.

The obverse or front of the coin is a three-quarter profile of the young Shoshone woman Sacagawea. On her back, Sacagawea carries her baby boy, Jean Baptiste. She carried and cared for the baby on her entire 3000-mile portion of the expedition with the explorers, Meriwether Lewis and William Clark.

On the reverse or back of the coin an American bald eagle with 17 stars around the eagle – one star for each state in the United States when the Lewis and Clark expedition began in 1804 – is shown.